think
like a pony

by Lynn Henry

Illustrated by Su Smith

KENILWORTH PRESS

To parents

It is recommended that parents read this book with children between 6 and 9 years of age. Children between the ages of 9 and 12 can read the book with or without parental guidance.

Parents and children will learn together:

1 How ponies see the world.

2 How ponies behave – and why.

3 How ponies learn.

Think Like a Pony is the foundation book for future books in the series. Through understanding the concepts explained in this book, children and parents will have the information and knowledge to equip them to learn the practical skills outlined in the series of workbooks comprising **Think Like a Pony on the Ground,** covering handling and ground skills, and **Think Like a Pony in the Saddle**, dealing with ridden skills with your pony.

Published in Great Britain by
Kenilworth Press, an imprint of Quiller Publishing Ltd

First published privately in Great Britain 2005 by the
author

British Library Cataloguing in Publication Data
A catalogue record for this book is available from the
British Library

ISBN 978-1-905693-09-2

Printed in Malta by Gutenburg Press Ltd

Disclaimer of Liability
The author and publisher shall have neither liability nor
responsibility to any person or entity with respect to any
loss or damage caused or alleged to be caused directly
or indirectly by the information contained in this book.
While the book is as accurate as the authors can make it,
there may be errors, omissions and inaccuracies.

KENILWORTH PRESS
An imprint of Quiller Publishing Ltd
Wykey House, Wykey, Shrewsbury, SY4 1JA
tel: 01939 261616 fax: 01939 261606
e-mail: info@quillerbooks.com
website: www.kenilworthpress.co.uk

Acknowledgments

I would like to thank everyone who has
been involved in making this book
possible.

My family, who have indulged my passion
for horses. Especially my husband Ged,
who is a constant source of support. Tom,
for his labour of love when typing and
advising me.

Su Smith for her enthusiasm and
wonderful illustrations which capture the
imagination.

Sue Cliff for actually making this book
possible through her untold hours of
precise editing. She has always
encouraged me in pursuit of my love
of the horse.

To my teachers and mentors Dave Stuart
and Sherrie Dermody who continue to
inspire me.

Finally, to all my horses, my greatest
teachers, and above all, in memory of my
beautiful horse, Willow, with whom this
journey began.

think
like a pony

Contents

The Author

Lynn Henry is a registered Equine Ethology instructor, living in West Yorkshire, with her husband and four children. A dedicated senior school teacher before leaving to bring up her family of three boys and a girl, Lynn has had a life-long passion for teaching, and particularly the teaching of children.

Lynn came to the horse world relatively late in life (35) as a result of helping her children to learn about ponies and riding and was immediately captivated by the relationship between human and pony. She has since dedicated 14 years to horse psychology, with particular emphasis on building a strong foundation on which to develop better understanding, harmony and friendship between pony and student.

Forever in pursuit of an holistic approach to horses, Lynn has added shiatsu for horses and iridology for horses to her list of ever-widening skills.

The Illustrator

Su Smith, Lynn's student and close friend, has been around horses all her life. A primary school teacher with outstanding illustrative talents, Su is able to capture the dynamic movement of animals and present them in a manner which is informative and inspirational to adults and children alike.

FOREWORD
by Carl Hester

When Lynn Henry asked me to write the foreword for this book **Think Like A Pony** I was delighted to be able to add my thoughts to what is a very special introduction to horse and pony behaviour. When I was young I lived on Sark in the Channel Islands and I had a very special friend called Jacko – who wasn't a pony but a donkey. Life in those days was a carefree existence and I learned all my horsemanship skills through trial and error with the horses on Sark and dear old Jacko. I didn't have a book like this to help me understand why ponies act the way they do and how to work with them in a safe way.

I have five godchildren – all boys – and this book is ideal for them. Even if they decide they don't want to follow my steps into dressage they will at least have a great knowledge of ponies – which can be dangerous to be around or ride if you don't understand them and they don't understand you.

If you dream of having the perfect pony who stands still while you get on, doesn't barge you out of the way to get to his field and would never dream of biting you, then you need to learn the language of ponies. This great book is easy to understand and is a must for any boy or girl who wants to be around horses and ponies. It is also great for non-horsy parents and will teach them a thing or two as well!

CARL HESTER

Introduction

We all love ponies – you would not have picked up this book if you didn't! Because we love them, we want the time spent with them to be 'the best'. A thing of dreams.

The truth is: ponies can sometimes be dangerous to be around or ride if you do not understand them and they do not understand you.

We have all dreamed of a perfect friendship with ponies. In that dream they never bite or kick. They are well mannered at all times, never thinking to drag you across the field to eat grass or to barge out of their stable because their friends have gone. When you appear at the field gate they 'nicker' with joy and come trotting over to greet you. They stand still for you to mount them and are willing to go out with you on a hack, confident that they are safe with you. They stop when asked; when ridden they would not spook or refuse to go through a puddle. They are eager to please when you ask them to perform any task. Jumping becomes fun, gymkhana a doddle!

When you are with your dream pony you feel safe with him and he feels safe with you. You can achieve anything together. These dreams can come true if you take the time to understand your pony, and see life from his point of view.

You may know what it feels like to be misunderstood. Perhaps you are trying to tell a friend, parent or teacher what you want or how you feel and they don't understand you or see things from your point of view. To understand your pony you have to see the world through his eyes. You have to FEEL and know what it is like to be a pony. It does not matter whether you have a pony or are thinking of getting one. Whether you think you know a lot

about ponies, or you think you know nothing about them. This book asks you to look at the world through the eyes of a pony, so you can understand how ponies think, why they act the way they do and what is important to them.

Through this understanding you can communicate with your pony and form a friendship where he will become a willing and happy partner. Time spent with your pony should be safe, using a language that you both understand. You can show your pony what is acceptable behaviour and help him to understand the world around him.

If a pony frightens you it is usually because he is frightened himself. If we understand why ponies are frightened we can help them to think differently about what it is they are afraid of.

You may know how to plait a tail or what all the different pony brushes are called. These things may have some importance in your world – but not in a pony's world. So, what is important in a pony's world? To answer that question you have to understand your pony, how he learns and what is important to him.

How does your pony make you feel?

First let's look at the friendship you would like to have with your pony. Does your pony ever make you feel any of these things?

Do you like the same things?

Do you both enjoy your time together?

Do you dream of the same things?

9

What does your pony think about you?

Is he pleased to see you?

Are you scared of the same things?

Take a little time to answer these questions.

Do you have any questions of your own?

These questions and answers are very important. You may have never thought about them enough before. Talk about them with a parent or friend before you look at the rest of the book. We do not always need to have the same dreams or like the same things as our pony, but we do need to understand what is important to him or why he is scared of some things. Without this understanding how can we make friends with our pony?

Most children want their pony to be their friend. They see their pony liking them as being more important than winning competitions or going out for rides together. What does it take to get your pony to be your friend?

To be a friend to a pony you have to understand him. You have to know what is important to him. You have to know how he learns about the world around him.

To understand your pony you have to see the world through his eyes.

Try to THINK LIKE A PONY.

Put yourself in your pony's shoes!

The rest of this book will help you to understand your pony and develop a friendship with him.

If you understand each other and you are safe, then you can have fun and achieve anything you want.

Friendship

What does friendship mean to you?

Do you listen to your friends? Do they listen to you?

Do they know when you are sad or unwell?

Are you
ever
afraid
of your
friends?

Do you ever feel bullied or threatened?

What makes a good friend?

Are they fair or unfair?

Are they fun or not fun?

Is it good to have a friend?

Most friends will be fun to be with, fair when you play, kind when things go wrong or understanding when you find things difficult.

Friends can be any age or size, boy or girl, family or someone outside the family.

What makes them your friend is that they care about you and your needs and you care about them and their needs. They are fun to be with.

The language of friendship

'To have a friend you must first of all be a friend.'
This means that you have to try to understand your friend.

- **What are they trying to tell you?**

- **What do they need or want?**

- **How do they feel in any given situation?**

To make a friend it is easier if you both speak the same language.

It is easier to communicate or talk to your pony if you understand his language – the language ponies use to communicate with each other.

Here are some signs that everyone understands

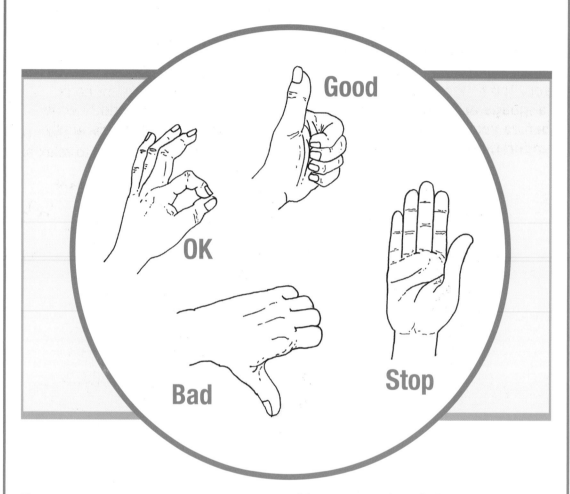

If you were to try to make friends with someone who did not speak the same language as you or someone who could not speak at all, what would you do?

Would you shout louder at them? Or would you try to find a way to help them understand what you want?

You can use hand signals or signs to show them what you want. Another good option is a smile. A smile is understood by everybody. It definitely doesn't mean I don't like you!

Friends will use their body language to ask for a hug or invite a friend into their personal space. Friends will feel safe being near to each other and will share close contact.

To make a friend of your pony you have to understand how to make friends with him using his own language.

This is one of the most important lessons when you are trying to make friends with a pony. It is your job to learn your pony's language and understand it, before you ask him to understand you.

Learning the language of a pony helps us on many levels. We can find out how they make friends, how they learn what is important to them, and how they deal with emotions like fear and love.

We have to feel what it is like to be a pony from the moment he is born, how he learns and how he forms friendships with his family and herd members.

From the beginning

When a foal enters the world he acts as if he were a wild creature.

He must survive by using his **instincts** and, later, what he learns about the world around him.

What are instincts?

When ponies act on their instincts it means they do not have to think about what they do or how they react. They just do it in order to survive. A foal may run from a stranger or a rattling bag. He does not think, he just does it.

The stranger could be another animal wanting to eat him; the rattling bag could be a dangerous creature wanting to sneak up on him. The foal cannot tell the difference, so to be on the safe side he runs first and asks questions later!

Through natural curiosity, trial and error and learning from their mother, foals usually work out what is safe and what is not. Whether a foal is born in a stable or in a paddock, the natural instincts that he is born with are so strong that he reacts to the world as if it were dangerous.

Without human contact the foal would live as a wild creature.

Instincts are very important for a pony. They help a pony to survive in the wild.

Why is instinct so important?

In the animal kingdom, ponies taste good.
They are fast food for many predators.
Predators are animals that eat other animals.
Predators such as lions, tigers and wolves all love the taste of pony!
An animal that is eaten by another animal is called the prey.
A pony is a prey animal.

Predator or prey?

**Prey animals are built differently from predators.
The boxes below list some of these differences.**

Predatory animals have

Eyes on the front of their head, which give good focus but limited range of vision.

Smaller ears that don't get in the way of eating meat!

Muscles that make them very fast over short distances.

Grabbing claws and jaws with sharp teeth to hold and kill prey.

Prey animals have

Eyes on the side of their head, which let them see all around.

Larger ears that can rotate to focus on sound.

The ability to run very quickly on long legs and maintain their speed over long distances.

Teeth to eat grass and vegetation. They have no claws or sharp teeth.

Using the boxes, can you see that humans mostly fit the description of a predator?

Let us think about prey animals

Think about a wild rabbit, a deer or a mouse. These are all prey animals. Do you think they are easy to get close to?

Do you think they are trusting of humans or other predators?

Can you think of any prey animals which are kept as pets?

These animals are not naturally trusting of humans because we are predators to them. **But**, if we learn to understand them and speak their language, they will trust us enough to allow us to love and care for them.

You may not think of your pony as a prey animal, but remember he was born with instincts that help him survive as a creature who might get eaten!

The senses

Senses are important to all creatures but especially to prey animals, who have to be constantly aware of their environment and looking out for danger. They have five physical senses, and some believe a 'sixth sense' of knowing.

THE FIVE SENSES

Sight

Hearing

Touch

Smell

Taste

Ponies and all prey animals live by their senses … They are very sense-itive (sensitive) creatures. If an animal lives through its senses it is in a state of constant alert and will find it hard to relax and respond to us.

If you think that your pony is 'too sensitive' it is because he is living through his senses and instincts and is expressing his feelings.

The senses and the newborn foal

As soon as a foal is born he must use his five senses and in a very short period of time be able to: **stand • drink milk • follow and respond to his mother.**

Mare and foal

When a foal is born he comes into the world in a protective sac, which the mother will lick away.
The first thing a foal feels is his mother's warm breath and firm tongue licking him rhythmically.
The first thing a foal smells is his mother as she sniffs him all over.
They use every sense to connect with each other.

REMEMBER
Sight
Hearing
Touch
Smell
Taste

Once the foal is standing, the mare will try to direct him with her head and neck. This encourages him, through feel, to do what she wants him to do.
She may direct and encourage him to feed. He will smell the sweet milk and feel for the teats between her back legs.

Later, the mare will suggest what she wants the foal to do using a wide range of signals. These signals are part of her body language.

After one or two hours the foal will be able to walk, trot and even canter, staying close to his mother's flank (side).

She will protect him and make him feel safe.

The mare has to protect her foal so that he will:

- **Bond with her and know that she is the one who will feed him and keep him safe.**

- **Begin to learn the language that he will need to communicate with the herd.**

A foal will call if he loses his mother. A mother will call if she loses her foal. The day after the foal is born the foal will be able to gallop and will have learned to lie down with co-ordination and ease. The foal will be very alert.

A good mother disciplines her foal and teaches him the 'rules' of what is acceptable behaviour so he can become part of the herd when he is a little older.

A very young foal must stay close to his mother's side. If he gets in front of his mother she may 'cut him off' with her head and neck, spin in front of him or even nip him.

What would happen to a foal in the wild if he strayed away from his mother?

Mares are extremely protective of their foals, often keeping other members of the herd (or even you) at a distance – sometimes for up to a week or two.

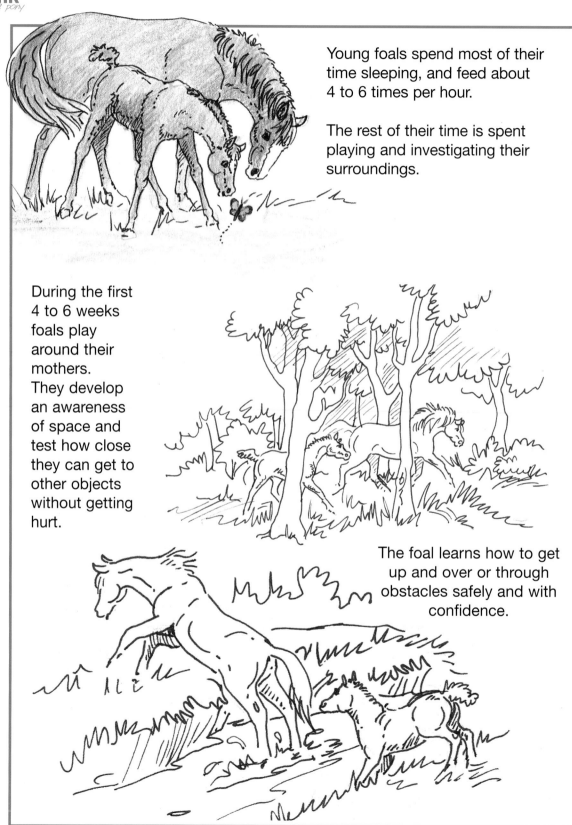

Young foals spend most of their time sleeping, and feed about 4 to 6 times per hour.

The rest of their time is spent playing and investigating their surroundings.

During the first 4 to 6 weeks foals play around their mothers. They develop an awareness of space and test how close they can get to other objects without getting hurt.

The foal learns how to get up and over or through obstacles safely and with confidence.

Foals love to play with their mothers, but sometimes they get too rough.

How does a mare tell her foal that this is not acceptable?

Body language

Ponies use some or all of their body language when they communicate and play with each other.

The mare may swish her tail or even nip her foal in order to tell him to 'back off'. She may even threaten to kick her foal.

Sometimes a foal is rough when he is feeding from his mother. A mare may swish her tail or raise her lower leg in disapproval.

A good mare always keeps her foal 'in check'. The foal has to understand that his mother will keep him safe, and in turn the foal must respect her.

All young foals need to:

1. **Be safe.**
2. **Play and communicate with each other.**
3. **Learn to be part of the herd.**

How does a mare teach her foal body language?

She nuzzles and licks him showing that she will not harm him.
She shows him that she cares. She makes her foal feel good.

She gently pushes him and guides him to the teats between her back
legs. He follows her feel and drinks her milk.
This also makes her foal feel good.

The mare will correct her foal at any time. She may nip him or swish her tail in order to warn him.

If danger approaches she will tell her foal to stay close by her side, pushing her foal and driving him away from danger.

This makes the foal **feel safe**, which in turn makes him **feel good.**

Foals learn the rules of play and language quickly. The foals practise these as they get older and their behaviour becomes reinforced.

Comfort and discomfort

If the foal does something the mother does not like, she makes her foal feel **uncomfortable** to let him know that she does not approve of his behaviour.

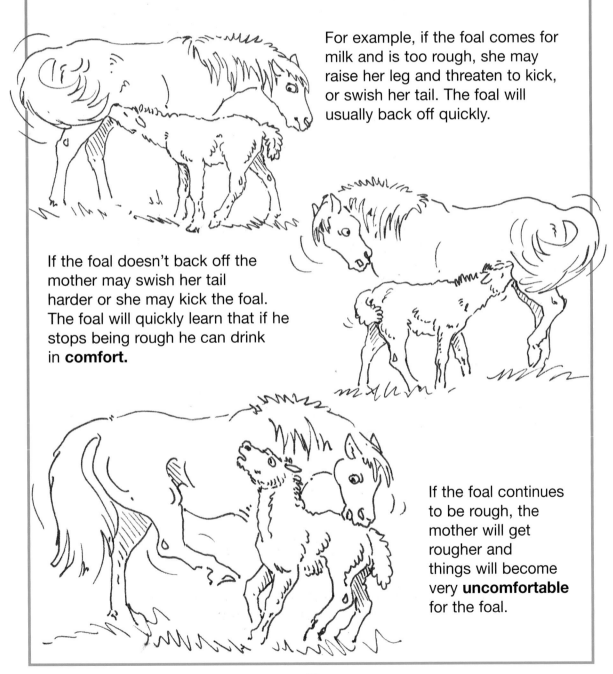

For example, if the foal comes for milk and is too rough, she may raise her leg and threaten to kick, or swish her tail. The foal will usually back off quickly.

If the foal doesn't back off the mother may swish her tail harder or she may kick the foal. The foal will quickly learn that if he stops being rough he can drink in **comfort.**

If the foal continues to be rough, the mother will get rougher and things will become very **uncomfortable** for the foal.

Ponies use **comfort** and **discomfort** as communication tools all the time.
They sometimes flatten their ears at other ponies.
This might mean:
 'I don't want you to come any closer. If you do, I will bite you.'

Ponies soon understand that if they ignore these warning signals, things will get very **uncomfortable**.

If a pony listens to other ponies and learns to make the right choice he will be **comfortable**.

In the herd

Play is the beginning of any foal's attempts to practise language. Foals use their bodies to communicate with each other. They get very physical and there is little or no verbal conversation, as we would think of it.

As ponies grow older they love to play more often. In the wild, youngsters spend a lot of their time playing. Colts like to play with other colts and can get really rough.

They like to race, chase, buck, leap, rear and wrestle.

These ponies are practising their skills. They are finding out about themselves and the other youngsters around them.

Finding out

Who is the fastest?

Who can rear the highest?

Who is the strongest?

Who can kick the hardest?

Who is the cleverest?

These young ponies are learning to assert themselves.
They are establishing who is the leader and who is the follower.

When you watch young horses at play it is easy to see them displaying leadership qualities. One young horse 'darts off' from the herd and the rest follow. The **'ring leader'** is the bold one. This is the one who will go to investigate anything new.

The leader of a group of young horses will often be the most cheeky and adventurous one. The other horses see this and will follow the leader. It is this **leadership** that makes a horse important to a herd.

These ponies are using their body language in 'play fights'.

Later they will use this language to establish leadership within the herd.

REMEMBER
They are practising their language so that when they want to use it, it will be effective.
They will be able to make themselves understood.

The importance of play-fights in the herd

**A HERD is a group of two or more animals –
one of which could be YOU!**

In a herd, whether it is in the wild or not, this 'play-fighting' is important. It is how a pony practises his language so that when he wants to use it, he will be effective and understood.

When ponies play they are trying to see if they can:

1. **Get into another pony's personal space.**
2. **Move the other pony's feet.**
3. **Establish leadership.**
4. **Make friends.**

Think of two strange ponies greeting each other.
They do not touch each other but pull themselves up to their full height in order to maximise their personal space.
They will often arch their neck and look impressive.

Sometimes they sniff each other left and right, and ask each other:
*'Who are you, are you a horse? You look like one and you smell like one.
Do I know you, have I smelt you before?'*

Then they often strike and squeal. This is to mark their personal space.
They mean: *'Don't come any closer, I don't know you yet.'*

Ponies will also play games to see whether the new pony will be let into their group.
They will ask: *'Who is the leader?'* and *'Can we be friends?'*

**REMEMBER THE MARE
WITH HER FOAL?**

It was important that the
foal stayed close to her
and followed her.
It made her foal feel safe.

All ponies and horses
understand this feeling so they
play games to find out who is going to be
the leader and who is going to be the follower.

Ponies play these games for the rest of their lives.
It is what they understand and it is one of the things
that makes them **feel safe** and part of the herd.

Listen to me!

What is your main way of asking or telling someone what you want?

How difficult would it be if you could not use your voice to ask for what you want?

You learn to rely on your voice when you want to communicate with others but you are always using your **body language** to exaggerate what you are saying.

It is difficult to speak without pulling faces and expressing what you are saying and feeling. Have you tried to tell a funny story and keep your hands still?

Could you let someone know how you are feeling by using body language?

What about looking at someone's face? Can you tell how they are feeling without talking to them?

Most of your communication is <u>verbal</u>.
Your **body language** supports what you are saying.

Most of a pony's communication is <u>silent</u>.
He uses his **body language** to communicate.

If you want to learn how your pony communicates with others, you must understand the body language signals he uses.

The pony's voice

Ponies have limited vocal communication with each other.
They use their voices to greet one another the same way we do.

Ponies can make several different 'calls' to other ponies.

The neigh

Have you ever heard a pony 'call' or neigh to his friends?
Perhaps when you are coming home from a ride, ponies call to each other or, if they have lost sight of the herd or a friend, they may neigh and call to each other.
A pony's neigh may mean:

- **Hello!**

- **Where are you?**

- **Is anybody there?**

- **You're back!**

The nicker

These are short, lower and softer than a neigh.
A pony may nicker:

- **When friends greet each other. (Does your pony nicker to greet you, perhaps when you bring him his feed?)**

- **When a mare calls her foal to her side.**

The squeal

Mares squeal when they are in season. When two strange horses meet they often squeal. This warns a strange horse not to come too close. It is their way of saying, *'I don't know you yet. Don't come any closer.'*

The snort

In the wild this is an alarm, or is used to scare other horses.
A pony may snort at something that scares him. A common example would be a plastic bag.
On the other hand, some ponies snort when they are excited.

Grunts and groans

These are sometimes heard when a pony is trying hard to do something and a lot of effort is needed (like getting up after a prolonged lie-down). A mare may grunt when foaling. Ponies may grunt when they are in distress.

Nose blowing

This is a soft, stress-free 'hrrrmmph' sound usually made when a pony is relaxed and comfortable. In fact it is similar to a human yawn.

Body language

Every part of a pony's body is telling you how he feels – what he wants and needs. You only have to observe a group of ponies playing together to understand the signals.

As a pony grows up, he learns how to use his body language to communicate, first with his mother and then with his friends in the herd. **Your pony will try to communicate with you in the same way.**

Ears and faces

Ponies use their ears and faces to let other animals know what they are thinking and what they are about to do.

A pony's ears are very expressive but often you have to look at the whole face to tell what your pony is trying to say. The pony's nose, lips and eyes are just like yours or mine. They are extensions of his five senses and show what he is feeling to the rest of the world.

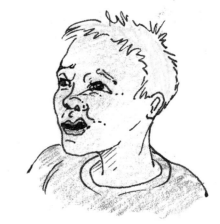

'Do you smell what I smell?'

45

Ponies' faces

Ears pricked, eyes focused: the pony is excited or listening to something in the distance. His body will be tense and his tail held high.

One ear forward, one ear back: the pony is thinking of two things at once. This one is listening to his rider.

Ears out sideways with a tense body: the pony is worried. His body will be stiff or braced ready to run, and his tail will be slightly up.

Ears flat back: the pony is angry. His body will be tense and he'll be flicking his tail. Sometimes a pony may put his ears back if he's in pain or scared; check the rest of his body language.

Ears floppy: the pony is restful. His body will be relaxed and his tail loose.

Foals' faces

Because foals are small and are easily hurt in 'pony-play', they make special mouth and neck signals to say to other ponies, 'I am a foal. I cannot hurt you, so please don't hurt me.' They will curl their lips, chatter their teeth and lower their neck to the ground. This is a movement that lets the other ponies know that the foal is not a threat.

Two foals playing together are no threat to each other.

'I'm just a baby, can we be friends?'

Head and neck

When a pony uses his head and neck it is a signal of what he is thinking and what he is about to do.

A stallion uses his neck as a weapon. He may drop his neck to the ground as a gesture that he is about to 'chase and catch you'.

A pony will extend his neck, drop it down and pull faces if he wants you or another pony to move. When a pony uses his neck, usually the whole facial expression is involved.

Ponies may also extend their head and neck upward in play to make themselves bigger than the ponies they are playing with.

It sometimes comes just before rearing.

Tails

When a pony moves his tail it is a very clear signal for everyone to see and understand.
When a pony wants to 'swat' a fly or irritating insect he will lash his tail to remove it. In the summer you will often see ponies 'swishing' their tails continually.
The fly is annoying the pony, so when the pony swishes his tail it is a sign of annoyance.
Here are some other examples of when ponies will swish their tales in annoyance:

When you approach your pony with his saddle:
Maybe the last time you put your pony's saddle on it was too tight. The pony remembers this and will swish his tail to tell you it was uncomfortable last time.

When you touch sensitive parts of his body:
Your pony may be sore or in pain and will swish his tail to let you know. He may feel vulnerable in these areas and swish his tail because he does not trust you yet.

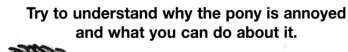

Try to understand why the pony is annoyed and what you can do about it.

Anger

More about tails

When a pony is frightened or meek he will clamp his tail tight. It may be impossible for you to lift it. The pony might even sink his rear end to the ground.
When the tail appears to go between his hind legs (clamped) the pony is very frightened. When this happens your pony may remind you of a dog that has its tail between its legs when it is scared or running away.

What could cause a pony to feel like this?

If a new situation is introduced to a pony too quickly or without understanding he may react with fear and clamp his tail. This could happen, for example, when a pony is mounted for the first time.

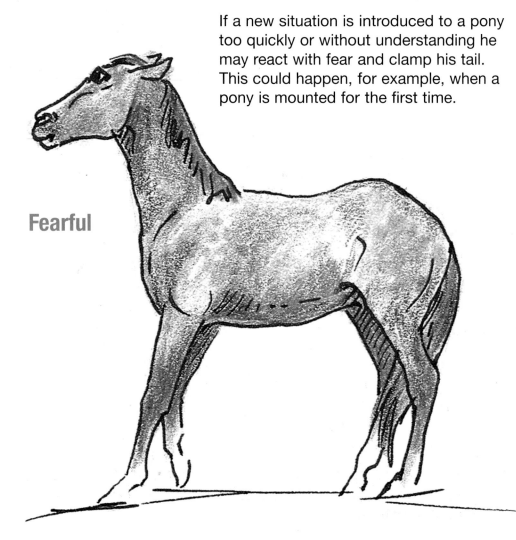

Fearful

The opposite of being frightened could be being excited.

Excited

When ponies are showing off and playing with one another, they will lift their tails high because they are excited and having fun.

Peaceful

Relaxing in the field. This pony is neither frightened nor excited. His muscles look soft, his tail is loose and his head carriage is relaxed and low.

Between being very fearful, very excited or very peaceful, there are smaller body movements which will help you work out what your pony is thinking and feeling.

Legs and feet

A pony will use his face, head and neck gestures, and then swishing of his tail as warning signals.

If these signals are ignored, a pony may kick or strike out with his legs and feet.

If a pony feels he needs to defend himself, he will kick out with his back legs.

He may attack another pony or even a human with his front feet.

A pony will only kick or strike if all other warning signals are ignored.

In summary

Just like us, if a pony is unhappy, frightened or tense he will hold his breath or change the way that he breathes.

The calmer the pony is, the slower his breathing, his muscles will look relaxed and his facial expressions soft.

If the pony is frightened his breathing will quicken. The muscles in his body will become tight and his jaw will become tense.

This pony looks tense.

This pony looks contented.

REMEMBER: Watching and being aware of all your pony's body language is how you will understand him, how he feels and what he is trying to say.

Personal space

Before you will let something or someone come close – into **your personal space** – you have to feel safe and comfortable with them.

You have to trust them and perhaps you have to like them as well.

Ponies are just the same. They know who they feel safe and comfortable with; they know who they trust and like.

All ponies are fussy about who they let into their personal space.

Ponies will not usually move into another's space without being invited. If they do, then they may 'play-fight' to discover their position in the herd and establish the rules of friendship.

When a pony invites another pony into his personal space it is to groom each other or to spend time together. It will feel good.

Ponies love making friends and usually have one special friend.

Do you know who is your pony's special friend within the herd?

Friends will often groom each other, play and graze together. Some ponies will even drink or feed from the same bucket of feed.

It is important that each pony has a chance to make a special friend.
It could be another pony.
It could be another animal.
It could be you!

Ponies love to feel the touch of their special friend.

Can I move your feet?

When ponies are playing or starting a 'conversation' with each other they want to know 'who can move whose feet'.

Why is this important?

Imagine there is not a lot of water to drink:
The pony herd is thirsty – they have travelled a long way to drink. The first one there will drink his fill and survive.

How do you think he stops everyone else drinking first?

You may not have seen a situation like this but you may have seen two ponies 'fighting' at a water trough in the paddock.
What looks like fighting to us is just pony play. One pony may even kick or bite to move another pony's feet away from the water.

REMEMBER: There may be no shortage of water in the paddock but ponies always act on their instincts. In the wild they need good instincts to survive. In the wild the pony who drinks is the one who survives.

If a pony can move another pony's feet, then he wins that move.
It is just like a game you play with your friends.
Usually no ponies get hurt, but the pony who wins
is often seen as the leader.

*'If I ask you to
get out of my
personal space
and you go, I will
not bite or kick you.'*

These games have rules and are fair.

*'If I ask you to
get out of my
personal space and
you do not go, I will
bite or kick you.'*

Ponies do not nag or bully

Ponies do not set out to use their strength to deliberately hurt each other – play-fights are usually for fun and to establish who is the leader.
Ponies can be very **assertive** without being **aggressive**.
The games ponies play can get very rough, but ponies always play by the rules.

When one pony submits to another and moves his feet, it is not out of fear, but **respect** because he has been beaten in the game.

If you are playing football and you want to tackle to win the ball, you may tackle <u>hard</u> but <u>fairly</u> in order to win the ball.
That is being **assertive**.

You should not deliberately <u>hurt</u> or <u>foul</u> your opponent to win the ball because it is outside the rules of the game.
You should not be **aggressive**.

Phases of friendly firmness

In any of the ponies' games, if one of the ponies gets injured, it is because one of them has not understood the rules of the game.

The pony who can get other ponies to move their feet is seen as the leader within that part of the herd. He has lots of moves he can use:

First he tries – **Wrinkling his nose and flattening his ears.**
If this doesn't work – **He'll lengthen his neck and toss his head.**
He might try – **Swishing his tail and humping his back.**
If this fails – **He will raise his leg.**
Before, finally – **Kicking or biting!**

Usually if a pony has had to kick or bite another pony, he will not have to repeat himself. Ponies tend to learn the lesson first time:

'I won't try that again, I'll get kicked or bitten!'

They take action to avoid getting hurt.

The assertive pony may only have to look or swish his tail in order to get the other pony to move his feet.

The pony who wins these play-fights or games is not always the biggest or the strongest. He may not even be the fastest or most athletic. Sometimes the pony who can outwit his herd mates or has more determination may win and become the leader.

Looking for a leader

All ponies are looking for a leader who will make them feel safe and comfortable. Every pony has the potential to be a leader. Ponies are born with these skills and develop them as they grow.

REMEMBER:
The mare is her foal's leader.

She made him feel safe and comfortable.

She taught him a language.

She taught him to trust and respect her.

Ponies want to be part of a herd

When young ponies interact with herd members, they play games to find out which of them is the leader and to make a special friend.

Ponies feel safe and comfortable within the herd with the leader and their special friend.

There may be more than one leader in a herd and leadership may change. There may be a kind of order in a herd, a first leader, a second leader, a third leader and so on. The first leader is the one the other ponies will follow more often.

If these 'leader ponies' leave the herd, the other ponies may feel less safe without them. In the wild it is the lead ponies who decide when to drink (when to stop at a water hole). When the herd does stop these leader ponies will drink first. The leaders decide when to graze and take it in turn to watch out for danger while the others rest.

The herd is their protection and their family.

Thinking like a pony

Are you afraid of a rustling
paper bag?
Are you afraid of crossing a stream
or stepping in a puddle?
Is a trailer a thing to fear, or a stable
a cause for concern?
If you jumped over a pole or ditch,
would it make you anxious?
Why would a pony be afraid in
these situations?

Think of the foal: he is naturally curious and will
investigate strange objects to see if they are harmful
or just things to play with. He might make
himself 'jump with fright' and retreat if he
feels scared. But he will approach the
object again, cautiously, to investigate it
further. All the time he is learning
about his environment.

This foal has discovered that the frightening
cone is a thing to play with, not a predator
waiting to kill him!

**REMEMBER: A pony is a prey animal and
is very sensitive to his environment.
A pony is always looking to avoid
danger to make sure that he doesn't
end up as someone's dinner!**

Who is going to eat me?

Why would a pony be afraid of a rustling bag in the hedge, when the rustling of a sweet packet excites him?

To a pony who is not thinking, a plastic bag in the hedge might mean danger. To him it could be a predator waiting to attack. This is a pony who is not thinking and is acting only on instinct.

Some ponies spook (shy) more easily than others. They may never have had the chance to investigate their world as a youngster.

Ponies learn by investigating their environment. They are naturally wary – but also curious.

They need time to think about and learn from each situation.

Do we stop them from 'thinking like a pony' in order to get them to do what we want?

Let me see clearly

A pony's eyes are set on the side of his head, giving good all-round vision to keep watch for predators. But this also means he cannot make sense of close objects straight in front of him – especially at his feet.

When a pony looks into water he cannot tell how deep it is or if there are predators lurking. In order to focus on what is on the ground in front of him, he must lower his head and neck.

If he is not allowed to lower his head so that he can see an object clearly, he may tilt his head sideways or even move his whole body sideways. We call this shying or spooking. We may think that a pony is being stubborn or silly not putting his feet in a puddle, but he has no idea how deep it is or what is in it.

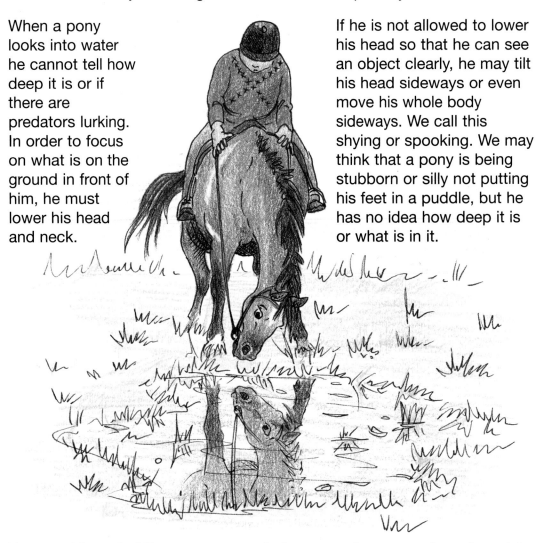

How would you feel if you were scared of water and someone forced you into it, allowing you no time to think?

Would you be afraid of water for the rest of your life?

How would your pony feel if you were to try to force him into water, before he had a chance to learn that it is safe?

I need to run

In the wild, a herd of ponies will only canter or gallop if they think they are in danger.

The herd will spend most of their time grazing, playing and sleeping; saving their energy in case they <u>need to run</u>.

If the leader ponies of a herd are spooked and start to run, then this is a signal to the other herd members to run.

They do not ask questions or stop to find out why they are running. No single pony would want to be left behind to be easy prey for a predator.

The herd may run for a mile or more before they stop and look for what spooked them in the first place.

This is why two or more ponies are reluctant to be separated, either in the field or out on a hack. They think – **safety in numbers**.

If one pony canters or gallops, then the other pony thinks he needs to run also – even if his rider may not agree!

The instinct to stay with the herd is very strong.

I need to protect my legs

When ponies are running on instinct they will often leap over obstacles they would never jump if they were thinking. Jumping over obstacles could damage their legs and with damaged legs they would be an easy target for predators.

Ponies are always cautious. Until they know that the obstacle is not dangerous, they will leap as high as they can.

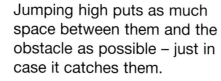

Jumping high puts as much space between them and the obstacle as possible – just in case it catches them.

This is why some ponies will leap over a pole on the floor, a small jump or a puddle as if it were dangerous.

If you watch a young foal crossing a pole he leaps until he learns that the pole is safe to cross.

Some adult ponies never learn these lessons, and will still approach poles or jumps with fear or leap too high to 'escape' over them.

Sometimes a pony is not trusting when you stroke his legs or pick up his feet. He may become tense and threaten to kick. This may be because he is in pain and protecting himself or because he still sees you as a predator.

Don't corner me!

If a pony is isolated from the herd for any reason he becomes easier prey for a predator.

If a predator can corner or trap a pony in a small space where there is no escape, the pony will be forced to defend himself in any way he can. He may be fighting for his life.

The pony may rear and strike with his front feet, or bite with his teeth, which were only designed to eat grass.

This defence is no match for sharp claws and teeth, so a pony in the wild will avoid being cornered at all times.

A pony who is afraid of small spaces is acting on instinct – afraid he may be trapped.

A thinking pony can be taught that small spaces can be safe places – for example: trailers, wagons, stables and narrow gateways.

Don't eat me!

If your pony does not want you to touch him in a particular place, it may be because he still sees you as a predator – someone he may not trust. He is protecting his vulnerable parts. Some ponies will not let you touch their soft underbelly. This is because if a predator attacks it could easily rip this unprotected area.

You have to build your pony's trust and confidence in your touch so he does not see you as a predator but as a friend.

I need to be with those I trust

If you have a pony who does not like to leave the herd to hack out, or who is nervous in competition, then that pony is telling you he does not feel safe outside the herd and his familiar environment.

Your pony may be telling you that he is not confident. Maybe your pony does not see you as his leader.

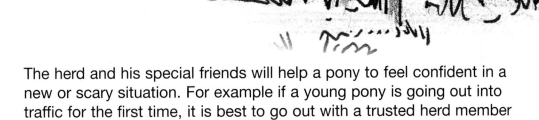

The herd and his special friends will help a pony to feel confident in a new or scary situation. For example if a young pony is going out into traffic for the first time, it is best to go out with a trusted herd member who is confident in traffic.

The young pony trusts that he will be safe if his friend is calm and a good leader.

Safety in numbers

A prey animal in the wild, outside of the herd, is an easy target for a predator.

Do I trust you on my back?

As you approach your pony with a
saddle does he look tense? Does he
have to move his feet?

Does he swish his tail or turn to bite you or the saddle?

When a saddle is on
the pony and you try
to get on, does your
pony move his feet or
try to walk away?

Look at a saddle and a rider through a pony's eyes
In the wild a predator would attack a pony by jumping on his back and
clamping its teeth around the pony's neck to kill him.
Your pony still has the instinct of a prey animal; to let a human, a predator,
onto his back or to take hold of his neck is a big step of trust.
If your pony moves his feet or objects to the saddle or you on his back, it
just may be that he is in fear of his life.

**The pony trusts you above his instincts.
You must not misuse this trust.**

Using a pony's language

Ponies use **phases of firmness** to communicate with one another.

There are many sequences and combinations of signals, but **every** pony has phases and warning signals.

Ponies will use comfort and discomfort to move each other's feet to resolve leadership issues.

The grey pony makes it very clear, using his body language, that the chestnut pony should move away.

The chestnut pony moves away and begins to graze with no ill feeling.

REMEMBER: Think like a pony and use his language to ask him to move his feet. If you use phases of firmness, he will understand and not hold a grudge.

Using comfort and discomfort is **one** of the ways in which your pony learns. It helps him to make the right choices.

Making a pony feel uncomfortable is **not** scaring or hurting him.

You will learn later how to build this language with your pony so that he can understand what you are asking of him.

Does your pony see you as a leader?

To get your pony to see you as a leader you must think like a pony.

You must defend your personal space.

You must be able to move your pony's feet.

You must be able to make him feel safe and comfortable.

You must be his trusted friend.

If your pony can move your feet easily – he does **not** see you as his leader.

If your pony can invade your personal space without being invited – he does **not** see you as his leader.

Why is it important to be a leader for your pony?

A pony who is scared will look for a leader to make him feel safe. A scared pony may run or bolt, kick or bite, barge or knock you over.

The pony is not 'being bad', he is only acting like a pony who is not thinking. He is scared and is doing what his instincts tell him to do. In this case – **RUN.**

Even if you have a halter and line (headcollar and leadrope) on your pony he may still barge into your personal space or **move your feet**.

Your pony may even take you for a walk!!

'I'm not moving my feet!'

'Oh yes you are!'

By understanding your pony's language you can move his feet before he moves yours.

You can ask him to stop outside your personal space.

You can then allow your pony into your personal space to show him that you are his special friend and that you can make him feel safe.

REMEMBER:
To be a pony's special friend you must earn his respect by showing him you are a good leader.

Becoming a horseman

The word 'horseman' is made up of 'horse' and 'man'. It means:

- **A person who can think like a horse or a pony.**

- **Someone who understands their language.**

- **Someone who understands their needs.**

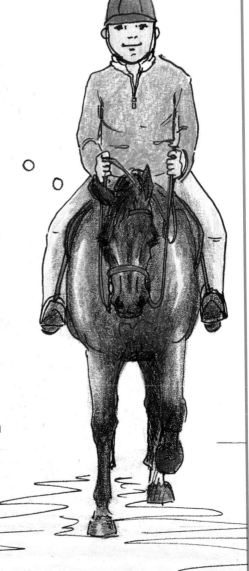

A horseman will ask a pony to perform tasks in a way the pony will understand and appreciate.

Ponies are very intelligent and if we communicate with them in a way that they can understand we can get them to **think**.

REMEMBER:
When a pony is <u>thinking</u>, he is much happier and calmer.

If a pony is afraid he reacts on instincts and may act without thinking.

If a pony <u>thinks</u>, then he may learn from a situation.

Let's think

If you are able to communicate with a pony so that he can think right down to his feet you are becoming a horseman.

This means being able to communicate with a pony so that you can get him to understand that scary situations can be learned from.

If we can communicate this we can overcome his first instinct, which is to run away from situations he thinks may be dangerous. If we can do this, we will be able to ask the pony to put his feet where we want them to be.

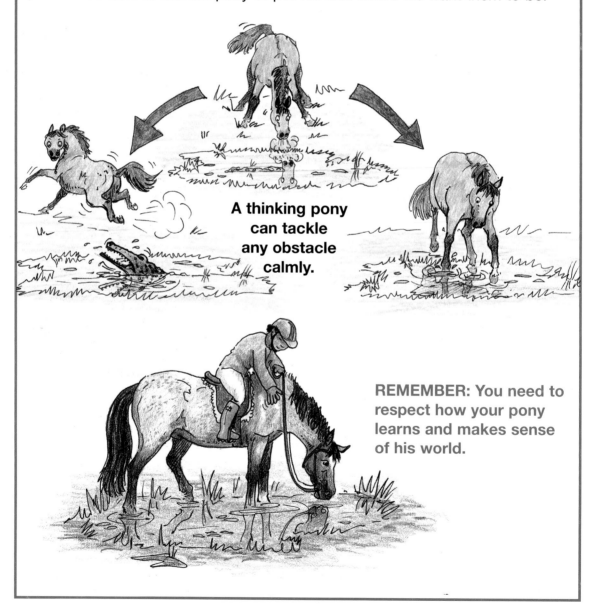

A thinking pony can tackle any obstacle calmly.

REMEMBER: You need to respect how your pony learns and makes sense of his world.

think
like a pony

Ponies do not always want the same things that you want

If you take the time to understand what is important to your pony, you can communicate clearly with him using his language.

Ponies do not care that they win a rosette or trophy.

Ponies do not care that they have the latest rug and matching accessories.

REMEMBER: Your pony cares that you are a good leader and a trusted friend.

So what do you do now?

Now that you have an understanding of why ponies behave the way they do, the next step of your journey is to learn the skills and techniques necessary to be able to communicate with your pony so he can understand what you are asking of him. You need to learn how to use body language.

In the next three books entitled Think Like a Pony on the Ground, Workbook 1, Workbook 2 and Workbook 3 these skills and techniques will be explained. I will show you the equipment to use, why you need it and how to use it.

When you have these skills, you can **safely** ask your pony to move his feet and perform any task with confidence. Have you ever thought of showing your pony that puddles are not scary, that plastic bags won't eat him, or that jumping can be calm and slow **before you get on his back to ride him?**

Communication with your pony starts with you on the ground.

You must 'Think Like a Pony'

so you can teach your pony about his world
and what you are asking him to do.

For further information please visit **www.lynnhenry.co.uk**

ISBN 978 1 905693 10 8   **£12.95**

ISBN 978 1 905693 11 5   **£12.95**

ISBN 978 1 905693 12 2   **£12.95**

Look out for these workbooks and the forthcoming THINK LIKE A PONY IN THE SADDLE series in saddlers and bookshops, or buy them direct from:

Kenilworth Press (an imprint of Quiller Publishing Ltd), Wykey House, Wykey, Shrewsbury, SY4 1JA
tel: 01939 261616 • fax: 01939 261606
email: info@quillerbooks.com • www.kenilworthpress.co.uk